SUCCESSFUL STORYTELLING FOR BUSINESS

How to grab attention
and communicate effectively
with any audience

Written by Nicolas Martin

Translated by Carly Probert

50MINUTES.com
PROPEL
YOUR BUSINESS FORWARD!
NETWORKING
Effective CV Writing
Resolving Office Conflict
Boost Your Concentration
Find Your Work-Life Balance
www.50minutes.com

STORYTELLING

- **Issue:** how can we use the popular technique of storytelling effectively?
- **Uses:** storytelling is all around us. Understanding the basics and successfully mastering the mechanisms to use it well is therefore essential.
- **Professional context:** job searches, project presentations, corporate communications, marketing a product or service.
- **FAQs:**
    - What is storytelling?
    - How is storytelling used in business?
    - How is a story constructed?
    - What risks should be taken into account when thinking about storytelling?
    - What makes storytelling so effective?
    - Where can I find inspiration for storytelling?

> "Storytelling is the foundation of communication."
> (Sébastien Durand)

Storytelling is far from a recent development. This "art of designing and telling stories" already existed in ancient Greece, during the lifetime of Homer (8th century BC). As individuals, we are, and always have been, more sensitive to information when it is told to us through a story.

But why is this? It is mainly due to the fact that stories appeal to our emotions and touch people in a much more personal way than any other form of message.

In our world of constant communication, what can be more effective than giving a story a little character and personality, in order to grab attention for just a moment? Amid this abundance of information, it can be difficult to find the information that we are looking for and, most importantly, to communicate effectively so that our messages have a chance of being heard.

Storytelling can thus make a substantial difference in both your personal and professional life, provided you master the key principles. You must strike a careful balance between the personalisation and broad appeal of your message, and between finding a method that can be applied and a "trademark" for you to develop. However, it is above all a creative and intelligent process that will be meaningful for both you and your target audience, in which you must never overlook the importance of the emotions raised by your message. Whether as part of a job search, a project presentation you are in charge of or a new internal communication technique, mastering storytelling will make your ideas more compelling and persuasive.

SUCCESSFUL STORYTELLING: THE BASICS

STORYTELLING: WHAT IS IT?

Although humans have been telling stories since the dawn of time, storytelling as we know it was not developed until the mid-1990s in the United States. At the origin of modern storytelling is Steve Denning (born in 1944), a communications expert and specialist on the subject, who rewrote his own story, not to mention his own legend, the "Zambia Story".

> "As a manager in the World Bank in 1996, I had been trying to communicate the idea of knowledge management and to get people to understand and to implement it. At that time in that organization, knowledge management was a strange and generally incomprehensible idea. I used the traditional methods of communicating with no success. I gave people reasons why the idea was important but they didn't listen. I showed them charts and they just looked dazed. In my desperation, I was willing to try anything and eventually I stumbled on the power of a story, such as the following:
> In June 1995, a health worker in a tiny town in Zambia logged on to the website for the Center for Disease Control in Atlanta Georgia and got the answer to a question on how to treat malaria.
> This was June 1995, not June 2001. This was not the capital of Zambia but a tiny place six hundred kilometers away. This was not rich country: this was Zambia, one of the poorest countries in the world. But the most important part of this picture for us in the World Bank is this: the World Bank isn't

in the picture. The World Bank doesn't have its know-how accessible to all the millions of people who made decisions about poverty. But just imagine if it had. Think what an organization it could become." (Denning, 2000)

According to Denning, in modern society, traditional communication has reached its limit, which has resulted in the total indifference of the public towards the majority of messages we see and receive every day. More specifically, he criticises the traditional trilogy of persuasive speech:

- stating a problem;
- analysing the problem;
- recommending a solution.

He suggests a communication trilogy that is more in tune with the present way of seeing things and is based on story-telling. This trilogy is based on:

- capturing the attention of the target audience;
- encouraging change;
- convincing through reasoned arguments.

The term "storytelling" is now used not only in the world of management, but also in politics and many other fields. This storytelling technique involves creating or re-creating a story that is based on actions and real or fictitious events. Whatever form the story takes, it always reports fact based on reality or an adapted reality.

The primary goal of storytelling is to transmit, to entice and to persuade through communication that combines information and emotion, reason and passion. Through this approach, the aim to give meaning to the link that will be created with the recipient is paramount, as is giving them desire to take part in this "great story". This is due to the fact that, in the end, what is more important in communication, whether professional or personal, than succeeding in touching the audience so that they retain the message with as little effort as possible?

TYPES OF STORYTELLING

Storytelling is such an effective communication technique because it plays on emotion. However, to create and implement storytelling, its scope and purpose must be taken into account. Although there are essential elements in any story, some sectors, such as business, have different requirements.

Despite the apparent diversity of stories that companies are continually projecting, Sébastien Durand, a consultant in communication and storytelling, groups them all into seven distinct types, which can be mapped out in the form of a weekly schedule.

DAY	KEYWORDS	ACTIONS	EXPLANATION
Monday (day of Diana, goddess of the moon).	Labour.	Overcome prejudice and be fairly recognised.	Like the moon which is illuminated indirectly by the sun, some firms are struggling to gain visibility, especially those that operate in complex areas, are not very "trendy", or work in B2B. They need to work hard in order to emphasise their added value.
Tuesday (day of Mars, god of war).	Conquests.	Conquer and adapt with agility.	Other companies are working to become a leader in their industry. They are in constant competition with their competitors and rely on flexibility and innovation to conquer their market.
Wednesday (day of Mercury, god of commerce).	Reassurance.	Inspire others and be close to customers.	Others aspire to become the preferred product or service of their customers, inspiring confidence. This is what they put forward in their communication. These companies therefore work primarily on their family rating, for example. But beware, trust and proximity is hard to win and is easily lost. Therefore, Wednesday's type is constantly in search of a consensus between the need to do business and the need to reassure customers.

DAY	KEYWORDS	ACTIONS	EXPLANATION
Thursday (day of Jupiter, king of the gods).	Power.	Be powerful and stay powerful.	This is suitable for large companies, such as multinationals or large institutions. It is suitable for brands whose power as indisputable leaders gives them time to let customers come to them, rather than go to their level to attract them.
Friday (day of Venus, the goddess of beauty).	Love.	Become more attractive and prompt desire.	Fashion and cosmetic companies, or even certain coffee or smartphone brands, aim to make the world more beautiful and young. Therefore, they want to create desire for their products and services by touching the imagination of their customers.
Saturday (day of Saturn, god of excess).	Sensuality.	Liberate the senses and break free from limitations.	Some companies target a particular audience over others, such as marketing directed at gay or ethnic minority customers, for example. Emphasis is therefore placed on originality, the specific customers, transcendence and liberating the senses.
Sunday (day of Apollo, god of the sun).	Knowledge.	Clarify and share knowledge.	Finally, publishing companies, newspapers and all companies that aim to distribute knowledge to people generally look for admiration from their customers on their expertise. But beware, the companies we admire are not always the ones we like…

These seven types of stories represent only a "narrative context", meaning a foundation, the starting point from which to build a story about a business. After determining what type is used, the model of storytelling becomes clearer, so the elements that constitute it, such as the hero, the obstacles and the solutions, are easy to include consistently and effectively.

CONTEXTS FOR APPLICATION

Apart from the business world, storytelling is used as a communication technique in many other sectors.

Communication

Communication means broadcasting a message. Storytelling is a communication technique, so this is where we will focus our attention first. It is worth recalling that communication has many purposes and applications, which can be seen in the domains discussed below and in its adaptation to specific situations which require different techniques. Here are some examples:

- institutional communication,
- internal communication,
- external communication,
- crisis communication,
- strategic communication,
- political communication,

- business communication,
- international communication,
- cultural communication.

Since it aims to go beyond descriptive and linear rhetoric, storytelling breaks from traditional communication, which relies on external, objective and known elements. It raises situations in everyone's mind that link imagination and reality, the individual and the global, and the personal subconscious and the collective subconscious. Storytelling therefore appeals to the subjectivity of the audience from the subjectivity of the speaker: the messages are designed around this basic principle. It involves serving a relational function and trying to influence behaviour.

Marketing

Just like communication, marketing is a relatively multi-disciplinary branch, which is found in both business and institutions. Storytelling therefore diversifies and updates the approaches and tools traditionally used in this sector.

Organisational life

Businesses rely on storytelling the most, whether for selling a new product or service, communicating new values or on an internal management level. Storytelling is used by companies to establish a new relationship or to share a story with the customer, not only to encourage them to buy the product or service.

Management and human resources

These two specialisms develop a particular relationship with storytelling, which allows them to emphasis the human dimension. It prompts the interest and solidarity of the teams around issues or projects regarding management, and it involves more employees in the company and its story in terms of human resources.

Politics

Political storytelling is very common, but also very controversial. Although it helps to promote the human and symbolic dimensions of society, it is often used for manipulation, with less virtuous intentions. When used wisely, based on a shared experience, it creates a relationship, and even a degree of confidence which makes a collective adventure possible. This can in turn reinvigorate the political field, which is often viewed negatively, and give new life to citizenship and the expression of democracy.

And many more...

Of course, other areas use storytelling, such as economics, medicine, psychology, journalism, education and social sciences. As it creates a new dynamic, it is and will continue to be used in many fields, especially in this new digital age, where an increasing amount of information circulates.

Finally, keep in mind that all of these fields of application of storytelling involve different targets – customers, employees, recruiters, voters, and so on. These should be taken into account when building a story, as it is these people who will receive your messages and it is with their emotions that your story will be interpreted.

THE ESSENTIALS OF STORYTELLING

Everyone uses storytelling, whether they intend to or not. It is therefore useful for everyone to be able to identify some essential elements of any story, whatever the field or target audience. It is these elements that make the technique and the communication effective, thus creating a different relationship with the message recipient.

Starting point

Logically, you should begin by defining the purpose of your storytelling, the "why I'm telling it". For example, in the case of a company, it is necessary to review the purpose of the business, meaning what it brings to society in general and how it responds to the expectations of its customers. You need to know your target audience. This will allow you to more easily identify the image you wish to convey, such as being an expert company in your field, being close to people, fun, modern, and so on. From there, list the items that may be turned into a story, such as the origins of the brand, its innovative side, the location(s) of production, the mythical figure of the founder, and so on.

You can now set a specific goal for your approach, whether it is to tell your brand story, modernise the image of a historic company, to give life to your products, enhance customers' brand experience, show that you are there and imagine your presence over the long term, and so on.

Initial construction of the narrative

Now for the construction of the story itself. To begin with, any story usually requires the following seven elements:

- one or more characters, ideally just one protagonist to facilitate the construction of your story;
- one or more locations;
- time, which can be continuous or not (jumps into the future and/or returns to the past);
- a plot;
- a narrator's point of view (character or external voice);
- a specific narrative tone (formal, informal, humorous, parody, etc.);
- a subject or theme that reflects the objective of your storytelling, defined in the previous paragraph.

THE THEME OF THE STORY

A good way to produce an original and memorable story is to let the character define themselves and define the direction of the story through their decisions and actions. In short, keep in mind the purpose of your story ("why am I telling it?") while leaving the message to form itself through your creativity as the story progresses. It is important not to stick to a specific theme at all costs, as this may cause you to fail to make the most of the other elements and end up producing an unexciting story. With this method, the topic will seem to come easily from the other six elements.

At this stage, these elements should be considered separately, without adding their content. For example, determine who the character is, but without thinking about their personality or behaviour just yet.

Moreover, there are three types of stories:

- stories based on personal experiences;
- traditional stories (which are, of course, reworked depending on your aims);
- invented stories, often from a combination of elements drawn from personal experiences.

Once the nature of your story and its basic elements are decided, you are ready to continue building your story in more detail and with more creativity.

Development of the narrative

Several steps have to be considered in order to advance in the construction and assembly of your story, through working on its content.

- Step 1: determine the quest. It is this quest that will capture the attention of your audience. Your quest will be partially defined by the plot and the type of story you have chosen to create. For example, you can rely on the Tuesday or Saturday type, defining an issue focused on the acquisition of something or based around liberation and surpassing limits.
- Step 2: characterise your protagonist(s). This is the stage where you give life to your characters. If you have decided

that your story will have many heroes, make sure that each of them has a distinct personality, behaviour or physical characteristic that will distinguish them from the others. Note that a protagonist can be a personified thing, such as your career if you are using storytelling on a personal level, or a value, a state, a rule, and so on.

- Step 3: choose the antagonist, which is the element that will come to trouble your character. This may be another character, a situation, an object, a value, a need, etc. Many elements can oppose the character, some of which you may not have thought of yet. Take the time to work on your antagonist, because without it your story will not be very interesting.
- Step 4: create the events that flow logically from the previously defined antagonist. The main character experiences several events that result in different feelings (happiness, sadness, anxiety, and so on), but these do not prevent them from advancing.
- Step 5: resolve the crisis and complete the quest. When the maximum tension has been reached, it is essential that an element untangles the knot created through the story. This element cannot come out of nowhere. Consistency is vital! Moreover, the story cannot end badly, since the purpose of storytelling is to spread positive ideas about you or your organisation.
- Step 6: revive the story. This step is really unique to storytelling. Although stories from films or books may end at step 5, your story, on the other hand, does not end with the completion of the quest. The listeners (your target audience) must be able to take it and spread it to other people. A good story is one that your audience wants to

tell other people.

- Step 7: come back to reality. Finally, it is important to relate the story to the person telling it (a politician, an association, a brand, an individual, and so on). Without this association, it is likely that your story will soon be forgotten, despite all the impact it had on your audience.

Now that the plot of your story is ready, it should facilitate the construction and assembly of the various elements. You are edging closer towards your goal! However, some "ingredients" are still needed to make your storytelling truly successful.

MUST-HAVES

So that storytelling does not remain a mere narrative, it must include some additional ingredients. Here are four elements that are vital to include in your story setting:

- A gripping start. The way you begin a story, like the way you finish it, is crucial to the effectiveness of storytelling. You have many options to begin your story, including the traditional "Once upon a time...". This introduction is probably very tempting, but be careful not to overuse it. However, that does not mean that you should never use it, as it can bring originality when used in a context other than fairy tales, such as a managerial story. Besides this famous formula, you can also start your story with "Imagine...", "This is the passion that drives me...", "I remember...", "One day...", "I always...", "Who hasn't...", etc. to be more original.

- Emotions. Storytelling is all about emotion: subjective and emotional feelings. This is what fundamentally differentiates it from so-called classic communication. A message is only effective if it is credible and the audience is prepared to grant the teller credibility. It is through emotions that this credibility will be granted. Therefore, keep your focus on building your story. The mind of your audience is almost like the canvas on which you are painting the story; ask yourself at every point what their reactions will be. However, be careful not to rely solely on emotions, otherwise your story will lose its effectiveness. As always, balance is key.
- Passion. This is understood as the "energy" that is essential to good storytelling. The passion you speak with cannot be solely your own (business, political, even personal), but also that of your audience. Since these are the people who will receive your story, you must convey their passion (for a certain business, a product, service, value, and so on) in a subtle and clever way, so that they can recognise it. You are often a tool to awaken this passion in them.

- Images and representations. The audience needs to be visually stimulated. They must be able to imagine the story and see it as it unfolds. How can you create these visual representations? With details that are familiar to them, by talking to them or by evoking situations or feelings that they have already experienced. Triggering these images in their heads is vital; just let their imaginations do the rest.

REVIEWING

Your story is ready. All that is left to do is review the details and answer a few final questions before telling it to your audience.

- Is the story clear, not only to the audience but also to you? While the audience of your story needs to understand it, it is vital that you understand it first. Telling a story is not very difficult, but without relating it to real life and giving it credibility, it is just another story! Therefore, you need to master it fully and handle it flexibly.

- Does your story meet its goal? When you are immersed in the construction of a story, you can lose sight of the initial goal that you set out to achieve with the technique. What do you want to achieve through this kind of communication?
- Does your story focus on its recipients? Ask yourself this question, because if the answer is no, you will not achieve any success, especially if you (or your company, organisation, policy, product, and so on) are the main protagonist of the story. It is not because of you, but because the story is about them that the audience will be able to identify with it.
- Is your story suitable for your target audience? Whether you look at the style, the nature of the story, the adventures or the characters, it is vital that these elements are relatable to your audience. It therefore seems essential that you understand who your audience is and what their concerns are. If you are not fully certain of the answer to this question, take time to analyse the issue again and fully review your story based on this fact.
- Does your story encourage people to tell it to others? If this is the case, your story is effective. The ultimate goal is for your story to make your audience feel that they have to share it with someone.

TELLING YOUR STORY

It is now time to tell your story and allow it to spread. Again, several factors must be taken into consideration.

The audience you are targeting will largely determine your distribution channels, since you want to reach it directly. However, be aware that the interconnections between all media channels are now increasingly strong. This means that you can combine different media and develop different content for each of them that will enrich the story, while promoting interaction based on the specificities of each type of media.

You will therefore have to adapt your storytelling to various formats so that it works for the various media through which it will be distributed. You have several choices available, such as the creation of a platform that centralises and delivers the story to all selected media or the successive use of several media platforms which take turns to tell the story.

Example of a transmedia campaign: ONLYLYON

The city of Lyon launched a transmedia storytelling campaign, with the aim of showing Lyon and its cuisine in a new light. The central character was a concept, the Chef Factory. It is a mysterious and prestigious school that has trained the greatest chefs and is at the root of many French culinary secrets. The plot is therefore based on real elements, but also has a number of fictitious aspects. A transmedia approach was developed over several years, using different media and in different cities, both in France and abroad. The content of the story was different depending on the media. The campaign featured:

- A film for international television, as well as the internet, available on a dedicated website and on some blogs to set the scene with background information;
- Street marketing campaigns in various foreign capitals (Brussels, Geneva, New York, and so on), such as tastings, games or competitions;
- An official Facebook page of the school to show the story on social networks, especially through the accounts of some students and teachers (Twitter, Tumblr, Instagram and so on). These conversational spaces were designed to enhance the various stages of the campaign and to establish a direct relationship with cuisine fans.
- Storymaking to supply the basic storytelling through a personalised kit available to culinary bloggers from different countries, so that they could write a story about their visit to the Chef Factory and contribute to the myth;
- Certain content reserved for the more curious.

TOP TIPS

- Storytelling does not tell your story, but allows you to use a story to your advantage. It is therefore a tool. This is THE golden rule that you must respect in all circumstances.
- Similarly, do not tell your story to yourself, but to your audience. They are the ones who will carry the story, and it is precisely this aspect of storytelling that is different from other communication techniques. Involve your audience in the story as much as possible, because it is an interaction between the narrator and the listener that keeps the story going.
- Capture their attention and surprise them, in a measured and reasonable manner. For example, a story will have more impact if it is connected to a key moment for your listeners: a current event, for example. The more you are able to capture their attention and pique their interest, the greater the chance of your story being passed on.
- Stimulate the imagination through metaphors, analogies and other tools. You must create visual representations whenever possible.
- Place emotion at the centre of your storytelling, without completely abandoning reason. Emotion is more than important, it is essential, and this is what makes storytelling different from traditional communication. The message recipient experiences emotions that will guide them differently.
- Adjust your storytelling depending on your chosen media. Feel free to exploit their diversity, varying the length

and format of your story. This will enable you to give it even more life and power.

- Do not limit your creativity. If you follow some basic steps with the essential ingredients, creativity will boost the originality or your storytelling, and thus guarantee its success.
- Spend as much time as possible preparing, but especially thinking about how your story will be deployed. As we have already mentioned, you need to make it your own, and then your audience will do the same.
- Think simplicity, authenticity and freedom so that your listeners can continue to tell the story with their imagination. If you focus on creating a buzz or talking about yourself in general, you risk your audience completely missing what you want to achieve.
- Accept that your audience will take your story, contradict it and handle it differently, and even sometimes reinterpret it. It is important not to restrict the creativity of your audience, nor do you have to limit your own. Who knows? Perhaps they will give you some material to continue your winning streak and achieve consistent results. You can then continue your storytelling time and time again.

FAQS

WHAT IS STORYTELLING?

There are different types of stories, each with different intentions:

- give meaning,
- gain visibility,
- improve or change an image,
- reassure,
- sell,
- create loyalty.

These intentions vary depending on the sector in which storytelling is used. It is clear that companies will often use it to sell, but this is not their only aim. On a personal level, you may wish to give meaning to your career or reassure yourself on the direction taken.

HOW IS STORYTELLING USED IN BUSINESS?

In business, storytelling is used for many different objectives, especially since the advent of Web 2.0. When discussing storytelling, examples tend to be drawn from the world of business, although there are many other fields in which this technique can be applied.

Companies have used storytelling extensively to:

- sell their products or services;

- communicate their story, mission or values;
- improve internal communication, particularly through HR;
- revitalise their management style.

HOW IS A STORY CONSTRUCTED?

Once you have a specific purpose in mind, building a story is not as difficult as it may seem. It should be a little creative, but it is mostly methodical and you must have a clear idea of the basic structure from the beginning. A good story can be summed up by: a protagonist, an issue, a problem, its solution, the effects of the solution and a call to action.

In addition, good storytelling allows the narrator to capture the attention of their audience by sharing a quest with them. The storyteller then continues their story by placing the protagonist and the antagonist, as well as the adventures and solutions. Finally, the story must allow the listener to draw a lesson from the conclusion, and must offer a logical association with the narrator so that it is well linked to their storytelling in the minds of the audience.

WHAT RISKS SHOULD BE TAKEN INTO ACCOUNT WHEN THINKING ABOUT STORYTELLING?

The main risk is telling a story simply for the sake of telling a story; in other words, creating a narrative devoid of meaning and interest for both you and your audience. It is therefore important to clearly define the purpose of your storytelling and stick to it.

In addition, there are two key reasons for the failure of storytelling:

- the narrative does not speak about the audience, but about the narrator;
- the story is based on logic and not on emotions.

It is also common for:

- too much importance to be given to the transmission of the message, which leads to the neglect of the "story" aspect;
- the link between the story and the message to be insufficiently clear;
- the emotional dimension to be poorly managed; in other words, there is no emotion or, conversely, too much.

WHAT MAKES STORYTELLING SO EFFECTIVE?

The effectiveness of storytelling when compared with other communication techniques is its emotional dimension and its credibility. The audience will feel more connected to the story because they can identify with it and apply it to their own lives.

THE EXAMPLE OF BRITISH AIRWAYS INDIA

A very evocative example of this is the British Airways India campaign, entitled *A Ticket to Visit Mum*. In this video, which is a little over five minutes long, a mother is seen in India and her son has lived in the United States for several years. They both express their desire: she wants to see her child, and he wants to visit his home country, in order to experience moments together. The airline, although mentioned, does not impose its identity too strongly. It merely constitutes an element in the story of these two people, which builds the plot and allows for the surprise. By watching the video, people living or who have lived away from their loved ones cannot help but imagine themselves in the place of the two protagonists. They feel certain emotions resurfacing and will want to share these feelings with others who understand. The story provides credibility because it allows for identification and appeals to the feelings of its audience. It is much more effective than a "Travel with British Airways to celebrate the end of year celebrations with family!".

WHERE CAN I FIND INSPIRATION FOR STORYTELLING?

Are you afraid that you are not creative enough or do not have enough inspiration to get started on a formal narrative? Look within and around you.

- Start by taking an inventory of what you already have: your assets, your experiences, and even your flaws. They can be a starting point, if not for your storytelling, to at least activate your creativity.

- Look at what is happening around you and what is being done. Think about the day before. Of course, do not completely copy what you find, at the risk of getting the opposite effect from the one you are aiming for. Tap into the inspiration in your environment and that of your audience. Mix and question what you see; this will give you a solid foundation and trigger the creative process.

OVER TO YOU

Creating an effective story is now within your reach. You have all the tools necessary to build a coherent narrative and trigger emotions from your audience. Still unsure about some areas? Here is a summary to help you connect the narrator, the story and the audience.

Narrator, story and audience

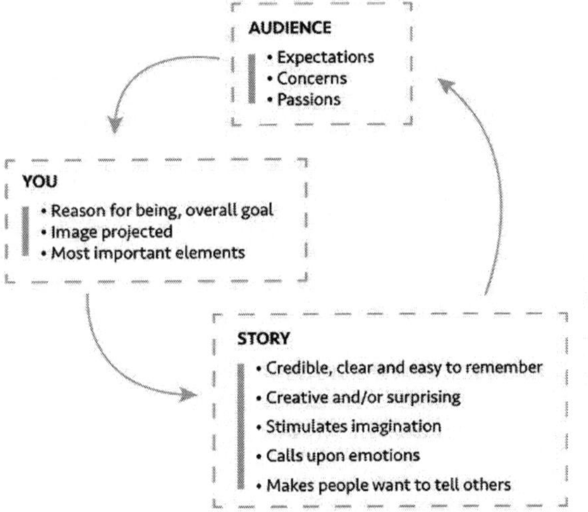

Great work!

We want to hear from you!
Leave a comment on your online library
and share your favourite books on social media!

FURTHER READING

BIBLIOGRAPHY

- Certon, N. (2013) Qu'est-ce qui fait l'efficacité du story telling ? *Cellie.fr.* [Online]. [Accessed 26 March 2015]. Available from: <http://www.cellie.fr/2013/03/20/storytellingnumeriquemarque/>
- Dangel, S. (2014) *Storytelling Minute*. Paris: Éditions Eyrolles.
- Denning, S. (2000) *The Springboard: How Storytelling Ignites Action in Knowledge-Era Organizations.* Hartlands: KMCI Press.
- Durand, S. (2011) *Storytelling. Reénchantez votre communication*. Paris: Éditions Dunod.

50MINUTES.com
History
Business
Coaching
Book Review
Health & Wellbeing
ISHIKAWA DIAGRAM
Material Method Machine
Mother Nature Measure Men
THE BATTLE OF AUSTERLITZ
NETWORKING
IMPROVE YOUR GENERAL KNOWLEDGE
IN A BLINK OF AN EYE !
www.50minutes.com

Although the editor makes every effort to verify the accuracy of the information published, 50Minutes.com accepts no responsibility for the content of this book.

www.50minutes.com

Ebook EAN: 9782806269911

Paperback EAN: 9782806284020

Legal Deposit: D/2016/12603/348

Cover: © Primento

Digital conception by Primento, the digital partner of publishers.

Made in the USA
Monee, IL
07 July 2026

56544687R00022